AMOR

Mateo Ríos

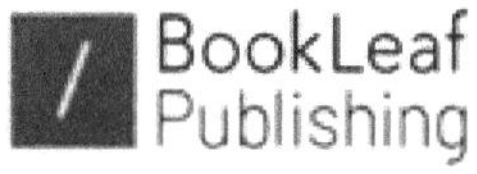

AMOR © 2022 Mateo Ríos

All rights reserved.

No part of this publication may be reproduced, stored in a retrieval system, or transmitted, in any form or by any means, electronic, mechanical, photocopying, recording or otherwise, without the prior written permission of the presenters.

Mateo Ríos asserts the moral right to be identified as author of this work.

Presentation by *BookLeaf Publishing*

Web: www.bookleafpub.com

E-mail: info@bookleafpub.com

ISBN: 9789357211307

First edition 2022

DEDICATION

This is dedicated to Taurean and Scorpio placements. May we experience all the love that we crave and deserve in this lifetime.

ACKNOWLEDGEMENT

Thank you to the astrology spiritualists studying our relationship with the cosmos and spreading the knowledge. Special thanks to Sam Aguilar who wrote the "2022 Eclipse Season Workbook: The Taurus-Scorpio Axis" which I referenced to learn more about these energies.

Sun

warmth, energy
I wonder if the Sun ever grows tired?
tired from providing life sustaining energy

everyone basks in the sunshine
enjoying the rays of light and heat

but no one asks if the Sun is tired of its role
everyone expects the Sun to be there
everyday, rising and setting

the day the Sun gets tired, chaos will ravage the
land

Home

For a long time I thought home was the place
you grew up in,
then I wondered why I felt so frightened to be
home.
Home is supposed to feel safe.

So many years I spent searching for a home,
somewhere to retreat to, a sanctuary.

I didn't realize that home was within me all
along,
building myself up brick by brick.

Allowing myself to sculpt the body I was meant
to have,
a body that protects me, that loves me, that feels
like Home.

Sensuality

I'm not interested in drowning out my senses,
becoming numb to my environment,
idly sifting through time.

immerse me into pleasureful sounds, music that
makes my heart flutter
her voice as she whispers "I want you",
the views of downtown lights from a distant
hilltop,
the smell of onions and garlic that make any dish
delightful
her soft cushion skin grazing mine as she sits on
my lap
the taste of sweet melon dripping down my chin

I refuse to experience anything less than what
tantalizes my senses.

Romance

romance is the expression of love,
it requires intention and observation.
it's not chocolates in a heart shaped box or a
dozen roses

it's gifting a book that reminds you of their love
and writing sweet messages on the inside cover
it's writing love letters using all the words in
existence to describe the love you feel for them
it's taking note of the things they like and turning
them into a profession of love

romance is timeless and priceless
if you want someone to feel your love, romance
them

Change

you anticipate it
like when you see a crack appear at the surface
of a wall
noticing it at first
but not paying much attention
until it starts to thicken
and it gets longer

you start to wonder, what if?
not knowing what's to come if the surface
breaks
how do you prepare for something you don't
know

it forces you to let go of control, which isn't
always easy
change is good, if you let it be.

Loyalty

changes can disrupt our perception of what once
was
it pushes you to re-evaluate everything
your values
your relationships
your path in life

it poses the question, what are you loyal to?
are you loyal to your wants and needs?
or will you keep pushing yourself to the
back-burner?

Jealousy

i shouldn't be jealous!
what do they have that i don't?!
who else can provide the way i can?!
how insulting to make me feel such turmoil!
the audacity to taunt me, as if I'm incapable of
dishing it back!
jealousy is contagious, watch yourself!

Speak

find your voice
and speak up
your ancestors have been waiting to hear you
your future self will thank you for it
those who listen are meant to hear you
pay no mind to the rest

Rage

I cried, ferociously.
I yelled to the top of my lungs.
Everything felt like it was shattering,
my heart especially.

I strained my vocal cords.
my ear drums rang,
popped from the amount of tension that my
whole entire head was enduring.

all the memories.
the confusion that they left me to sift through,
just to find out that it was all a lie.

FOOL!

How many times am I going to re-live this?
How many times will I allow my illusions to
cloud my intuition?
How many times will I allow myself to be
treated like a fool?,
when I know I'm a KING!

Moon

phases, cycles

because of her the future is never certain
whirling the depths of our emotions
testing, testing, testing

darker paths are illuminated
which way will the waves carry you?
will you fight it?
can you?

Yearning

There are days when all I do is think about you
today is one of them
and the day before
and most likely tomorrow too
I've been here before
yearning

I miss holding you with my gaze,
the intensity of our souls connecting,
recognizing each other as if it's been ages.

time stops.
everything is in slow motion
it's as if we're the only two people in the room
I look away each time
in fear of revealing my true feelings for you
I've been here before
yearning

I don't like having my feelings put on pause
stagnancy makes me anxious
as if I'm holding a part of myself back
shutting myself out
yearning to shout my love for you
and hold you in my arms.

it's easier,
to pretend that we don't have something real.

when you make the move
I'll be ready to move with you.

Seduction

She ignites the fiery hells within me
my horns burst through my skin at the flashing
images of her eyes

my arm wrapping her tightly against me with my
hand around her neck
just enough pressure to feel the vibrations of her
moans
my hand sinking below her belly, slipping into
her throbbing lips
juices and goosebumps, juices and goosebumps

the mirror puts us on display
our eyes lock
I moan out her name

it always feels so real

Secrets

whispers
words at the tips of tongues
messages never delivered
feelings buried beneath the weight of reality
hidden truths tucked away in the darkest of
corners
can you trust anyone to keep them for you?

Possession

what's mine is not yours, it's mine
if I claim you, you're mine
you and everyone around you will be reminded
of that
no moment will pass where I'm not
in your thoughts
in your presence
in your subconscious
you are a treasure
a treasure worthy of worship from all those who
cross your path
but you are still mine

Intuition

a fleeting thought at first
a feeling lingers
something you know but can't quite explain
where does this knowing come from?

doubt floods in
but you already know
it's been proven to you before
let your inner knowing guide you

Transformation

they don't tell you that when you bloom
there will be those who secretly hate you for it
"how dare you change and become a better
version of yourself!"
what they're really saying is "how dare you
leave me behind!"

transformation is a lonely process,
one worth embracing.

Death

have you ever witnessed someone's last breath?
felt the skin that was once warm, now ice cold
eye lids closed, transported into another realm
silence creeps in before the impending wailing

some people long for it,
fighting themselves to keep from meeting with
Death.
meet Death when you are meant to,
because Life is unpredictable, but Death is
certain.

Nostalgia

life keeps going
memories are all we are left with

the sound of their laugh
the way their fingers scraped the grinder for
residue
the scent of the shampoo she used
the way he howled when the Dodgers scored a
run
the looks she would give you from across the
room
the jokes you busted out laughing too, and the
ones that weren't funny

it's not fair, to miss moments that have passed
longing to relive them, maybe even have the
chance to say something different
to live in a constant state of nostalgia is
bittersweet.

www.ingramcontent.com/pod-product-compliance
Lightning Source LLC
LaVergne TN
LVHW050305200726
843509LV00015B/3172